MAY   2007

0438 77936

CH

animals**animals**

Kangaroos
by **Judith Jango-Cohen**

mc **Marshall Cavendish**
Benchmark
New York

To Carole, friend and fellow writer

The author thanks Doug Sanders, editor, for his careful and skillful review.

Series consultant
James G. Doherty
General Curator, Bronx Zoo, New York

Marshall Cavendish Benchmark
99 White Plains Road
Tarrytown, NY 10591-9001
www.marshallcavendish.us

Library of Congress Cataloging-in-Publication Data

Jango-Cohen, Judith.
Kangaroos / by Judith Jango-Cohen.— 1st ed.
p. cm. — (Animals, animals)
Summary: "Describes the physical characteristics, behavior, and habitat of kangaroos"—Provided by publisher.
Includes bibliographical references and index.
ISBN 0-7614-1869-5
1. Kangaroos—Juvenile literature. I. Title. II. Series.

QL737.M35J36 2005
599.2'22—dc22
2004021621

Photo research by Joan Meisel

Cover photo: Christine Bull

The photographs in this book are provided by permission and through the courtesy of: *Animals Animals:* Gerard Lacz, 12;
Juergen & Christine Sohns, 26; Howie Garber, 34. *Bruce Coleman, Inc.:* Daniel Zupanc, 9 (bottom); Hans Reinhard, 22;
Norman Owen Tomalin, 36. *Christine Bull:* 1, 4, 10, 19, 20, 24, 31, 41, 42. *Corbis:* Martin Harvey, 15. *Peter Arnold, Inc.:*
Roland Seitre, 7, 14; Ruoso Cyril, 32; Martin Harvey, 40. *Photo Researchers, Inc.:* Wayne Lawler, 8; Will & Deni McIntyre,
9 (top); Martin Harvey, 25; Art Wolfe, 28; George Bernard, 39.

Series design by Adam Mietlowski

Printed in China

1 3 5 6 4 2

Contents

1 Introducing Kangaroos

A baby red kangaroo springs in the grass like a bouncy windup toy. It jumps onto its mother's back, flips over, and then swats its mother's ears. The mother takes hold of her *joey* and tries to quiet it. She licks its face and neck.

Nearby, a wedge-tailed eagle rustles its broad black wings and launches into the air. At the sight of this *predator*, the mother kangaroo calls, "Chuck! Chuck!" Instantly, the joey tumbles into its mother's pouch. Hidden in the deep pocket, only its two big hind feet stick out.

Big-footed, bouncing kangaroos live in Australia, including the island of Tasmania. They are also found

A baby kangaroo can graze on grass while relaxing in its mother's pouch.

in New Guinea, a neighboring island to the north. Through the years, people have brought kangaroos into places outside their natural homelands. Now wild kangaroos also live in New Zealand, Great Britain, and Hawaii.

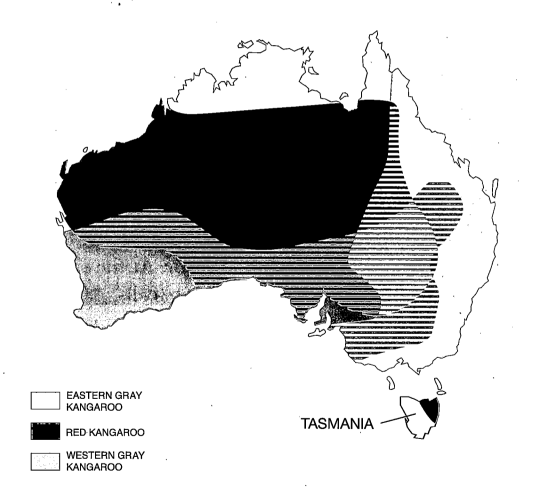

EASTERN GRAY KANGAROO

RED KANGAROO

WESTERN GRAY KANGAROO

TASMANIA

Kangaroos have adapted well to life in Australia—the mammal's homeland.

6

There are about sixty-nine *species*, or kinds, of kangaroos. Scientists do not agree on the exact number. The most common kangaroos are the red, eastern gray, and western gray. These animals are the largest of the kangaroos. Males may weigh 200 pounds (91 kilograms). Females weigh about half as much. Other members of the kangaroo family include tree-kangaroos, wallabies, wallaroos, bettongs, and rat-kangaroos. The musky rat-kangaroo is the smallest species. It weighs just 1 pound (454 grams) and is the only kangaroo that does not hop.

Yellow-footed rock-wallabies gracefully bounce from boulder to boulder.

Species Chart

Male red kangaroos are usually rusty brown, but most females are grayish blue.

Eastern gray kangaroos have long, soft, gray-brown fur.

Western gray kangaroos live throughout southern Australia. Some scientists have suggested changing their name to the southern gray kangaroo.

A kangaroo's back teeth gradually wear down from grinding coarse grasses.

Kangaroos make their homes in a variety of *habitats.* Red kangaroos live mostly in hot, dry grasslands. Eastern gray and western gray kangaroos are drawn to shady woodlands. Sunny piles of boulders are the habitat of nimble rock-wallabies. These kangaroos also find shelter from the heat in cool rocky caves. Tree-kangaroos are well suited to the humid rain forest. They spring like acrobats from tree to tree. Musky rat-kangaroos also live in the rain forest. But they stay on the ground, building leafy nests on the forest floor. Burrowing bettongs prefer life underground. These kangaroos scratch out deep burrows in desert areas.

Despite their differences, kangaroo species are similar in several ways. All kangaroos are *marsupials.* Marsupials give birth to young that are not fully developed. Most female marsupials have a pouch where the newborn continues to grow and develop. All kangaroos feed mainly on plants. They have long tails, strong legs, and large feet. Kangaroos have hand-like, clawed paws but no thumbs. They use their tails for balance and their hind legs to hop.

2 Cruising Kangaroos

As the setting sun turns the clouds cotton candy pink, two gray kangaroos leap through a valley. They glide through glowing grass, up and down, like creatures on a carousel. One kangaroo has a joey aboard. The baby pokes its head out of the pouch and watches the meadow whiz by.

Kangaroos are the largest hopping animals. They are equipped with muscular hind legs and huge padded feet. Each foot has an enormous middle toe that bears most of the kangaroo's weight. To leap forward, a kangaroo bends its hind legs and pushes off on both feet. While coasting through the air, it stretches out its long legs. When the kangaroo lands,

In the 1700s, a European explorer noted that kangaroos hopping over rocky ground easily beat his greyhound.

13

both legs are straight. But it quickly bends them for the next powerful push-off. The tail helps to steady the kangaroo so it does not tip too far forward.

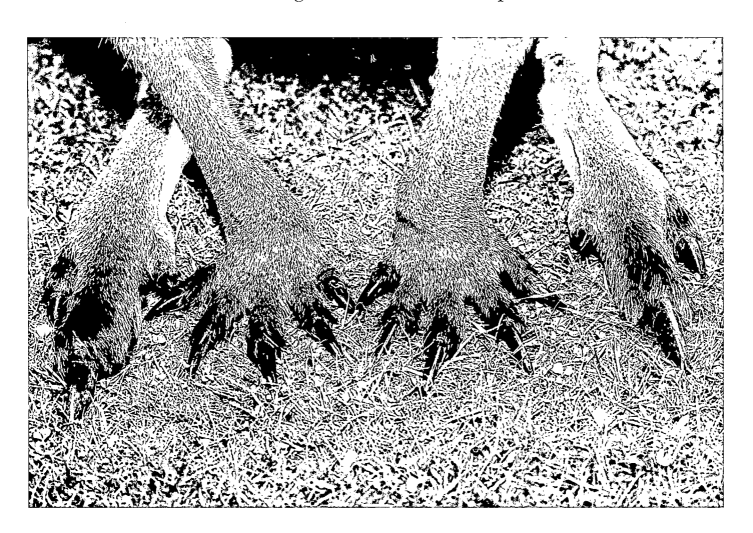

Kangaroos comb their fur with the two claws growing closely together on their hind feet.

A scientific study showed that a group of five dingoes killed eighty-three red kangaroos in a seven-week period.

A kangaroo's springy hops are powered by elastic tissues called *tendons.* Tendons connect bones to the muscles that move them. With their rubbery tendons, leaping kangaroos use less energy than animals that run on four legs. This means they get tired less quickly. Predators, such as the wild dogs called dingoes, cannot keep pace with racing kangaroos.

The Kangaroo:

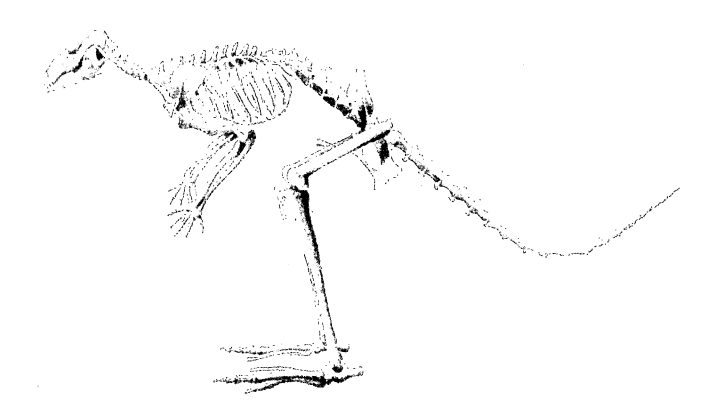

Long hind legs—and the powerful muscles attached to them—make a kangaroo . . .

Inside and Out

. . . perfectly designed for hopping. The thick tail helps provide balance.

Kangaroos have a special way of breathing that saves them energy when they hop. When an animal like a dingo runs, it uses energy to move the chest muscles that help it to breathe. A kangaroo's body works differently. When its feet push off from the ground, air is then pumped out of its lungs. As its legs stretch forward, the lungs expand and fill. Since a kangaroo's chest muscles are not needed to move air in and out, it saves energy while hopping.

Red kangaroos usually move at a speed of about 15 miles (24 kilometers) per hour. If they are being chased and need to pick up the pace, they increase the length of each hop. The hopping rate, or the number of hops per minute, stays the same. To hop faster than 21 miles (34 kilometers) per hour, however, they must also increase their hopping rate. A scientist studying red kangaroos clocked a racing kangaroo at 31 miles (50 kilometers) per hour. At that speed, the kangaroo was touching down about once every 23 feet (7 meters).

While hopping leisurely, or while escaping a predator, kangaroos spring forward more than up and down. But when faced with an obstacle such as

Scientists study how kangaroos move by training them to hop on a treadmill.

Four eyes are better than two when watching for danger.

a bush, boulder, or fence, kangaroos can easily leap up and over it. They have been seen vaulting over 10-foot (3-meter) fences. This ability gives them an edge over their predators.

Kangaroos bound away at the first sign of trouble. The sooner a kangaroo detects danger, the better chance it has of escaping. That is why kangaroos are always on the alert—looking, listening, and sniffing.

Did You Know . . .

Kangaroos are not constantly leaping around. Sometimes they "walk." Balancing on their front legs and tail, they swing both back legs forward. Then, planting their hind legs, they move their two front legs up.

3 Life in the Mob

Ribbons of fog trim the smooth, blue mountaintops of eastern Australia. Eastern gray kangaroos, with heads bowed, graze on the open slopes. Gripping tufts of grass with their front teeth, they rip them off with a yank of their heads. Their back molars, lined with ridges, help to chop up the tough stalks.

On some days, as the morning grows warm, a wind tickles the kangaroos' whiskers and rumples their fur. Feathery grass stalks flutter, and leafy limbs sway and shudder. On these blustery days, the kangaroos cut short their breakfast on the ridge and bound down the slopes. Soon the entire *mob* has left its feeding ground and is gathered in the valley below.

In large groups, each kangaroo can spend less time watching for predators and more time eating.

Water holes are the most common place for predators to attack kangaroos.

High ridges are not as sheltered from whipping winds as low-lying valleys. But the valley is safer for another reason. Whistling breezes mask sounds that may signal danger. Settled in the open valley, the kangaroos can view the hillside for approaching dingoes. As a mob, rather than in smaller groups, kangaroos have more eyes on the alert.

One gusty day, a mob of eastern gray kangaroos settles into a valley. The last kangaroo to arrive is a muscular male with tattered ears. He struts on his toes to show off his height. Walking past the lounging groups he expects each male to jump to its feet and honor him with a "cough." By giving a hoarse "Aarrh! Aarrh!" each is saying that the large kangaroo is the top male, the *dominant* member of the mob.

One male, about the same size, but two years younger, decides not to get up or "cough." The older kangaroo does not ignore this insult. He challenges his rival by leaning forward and rubbing his chest on a patch of grass. This "chest swiveling" deposits his scent. As a final touch, he urinates on the grassy clump. The younger kangaroo leisurely rests on one elbow. He does not rise but instead offers a short, "Aarrh! Aarrh!" The day may be too hot to pick a fight.

Young male eastern gray kangaroos practice "boxing" with each other.

Balancing on its tail, a kangaroo delivers a solid kick to its rival.

About a week later the two meet again. The dominant kangaroo comes upon the younger male, who is following a female. The right to mate with females belongs to the dominant male alone. The younger male decides to battle the older one. The two kangaroos crouch and face each other. As if at some silent signal, they leap up. Grappling with their forelegs, they try to push each other to the ground. Leaning back on their muscular tails, they kick each other with both hind legs.

Dust and fur swirl around the dueling males. The older male wrestles the younger kangaroo to the ground. But the fallen kangaroo rolls over and jumps up. He delivers three solid kicks to his opponent. But the dominant male rallies and gets a stranglehold on the other. Tiring, the younger kangaroo "coughs" and hops away.

The two kangaroos are so close in size and strength that the rivalry continues for months. In an unusual compromise, both kangaroos end up sharing the females. Each holds mating rights with the twenty females in his area. When the joeys are born, the males will take no part in raising them. That is the job of the mothers.

Did You Know . . .

Kangaroos try to keep cool by stretching out in the shade. If they get overheated, they start to pant, and drool dribbles from their mouths. Kangaroos wipe or lick this saliva onto the inside of their forelegs. The fur is thin there, and many tiny blood vessels lie close to the skin. As moisture on the forelegs absorbs heat from the blood, the water *evaporates*, cooling the kangaroo.

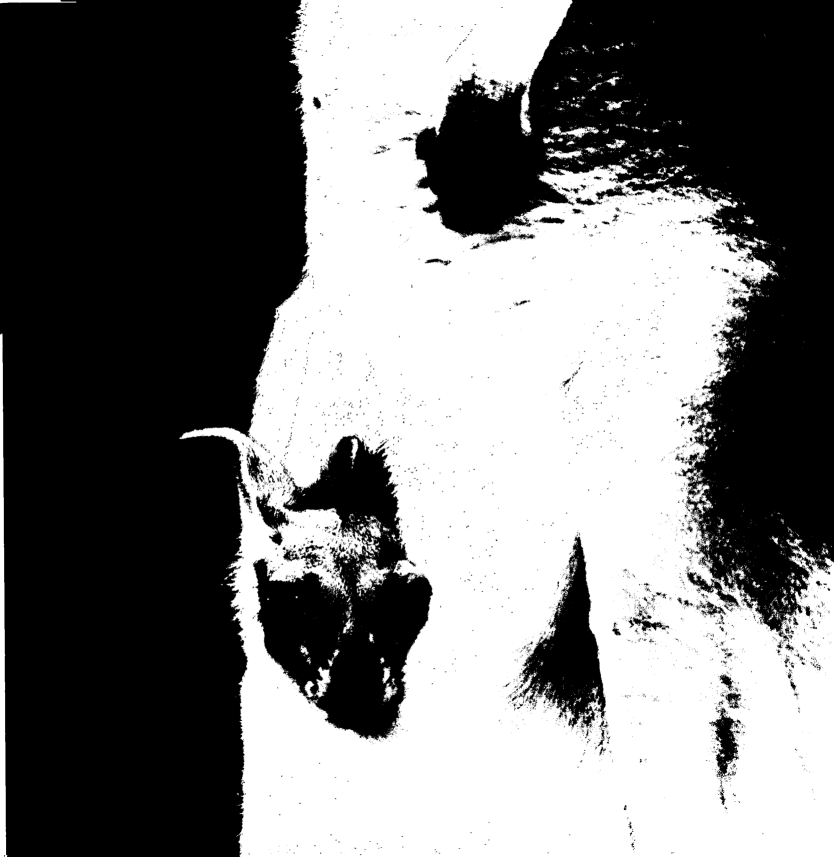

4 Growing Joeys

A female eastern gray kangaroo pulls open her empty pouch with both forepaws and pokes her nose inside. She begins licking the pouch clean as she has been doing for two days. Soon a tiny pink creature emerges from an opening near her tail. It is enclosed in a clear, fluid-filled sac. The newborn rips open the sac with the sharp claws on its forepaws. Except for its tiny forelimbs, the newborn kangaroo looks like a slimy, pink worm. It is hairless, and its eyes, ears, hind legs, and tail have not yet developed.

Clutching the mother's thick fur with its fore-limbs, the newborn *instinctively* heads upward toward its mother's pouch. After about three minutes

A kangaroo mother keeps her joey tucked in by tightening her pouch muscles.

of climbing, it reaches the rim of the pouch. Crawling inside, the sightless newborn finds a nipple and latches on. Most likely it locates the nipple using its senses of smell and touch. Like all *mammals*, the joey's first meal is its mother's milk.

For the next eight months the baby stays tucked inside this cozy pocket, sleeping and drinking. Red kangaroos, which develop and grow faster than gray kangaroos, leave the pouch for the first time at about six months. The pouch provides warmth and shelter. A waxy substance produced inside the pouch keeps the baby's skin moist. The mother sees little of her baby unless an ear or leg pokes out of the pouch. Once in a while she peeks inside and cleans away the baby's waste.

Then the day arrives when the baby's leisurely life comes to an abrupt end. The mother relaxes her pouch muscles, and the joey comes tumbling out. This introduction to the outside world usually ends seconds later as the baby scrambles back to the safety of the pouch. During the next two months, the joey gets bolder and begins to explore outside the pouch. It tries out its lanky legs and samples the grass. Among the taller stalks, only the tips of its ears can be seen, popping up and down.

As the joey grows older, it can feed directly from the warmth and safety of its mother's pouch.

A frisky eastern gray joey does not give its mother much rest.

But the mother knows where her joey is at all times. She also keeps an eye out for predators. At the sight of a cruising eagle or a prowling dingo, the mother's urgent call signals the joey. It quickly returns to the pouch. Joeys that stray too far from their mothers can fall prey to these skillful hunters.

Eventually a baby grows too big for the pouch. The joey may not think so, but its mother does. She tightens her pouch muscles and locks her baby out. When this happens, a joey may panic and head for another mother's pouch. If the other female has her own joey inside, she may attack the young intruder. To prevent this, a mother keeps her joey away from other kangaroos until it gets used to its new independence.

Although a joey no longer climbs into its mother's pouch, it sometimes sticks its head in for comfort. It continues to drink its mother's milk by standing outside. Gray kangaroo joeys nurse until they are eighteen months old. This is eight months after they have left the pouch for good. Red kangaroos nurse outside for four months, until they are about a year old. Mother kangaroos usually give birth again shortly after their pouch becomes empty.

Even after leaving the pouch, young kangaroos stay near their mothers—lying, feeding, and playing with them.

While a joey is nursing from outside, another baby is nursing inside the pouch from a different nipple.

After leaving the protection of the pouch, joeys follow their mothers and watch them closely. Young kangaroos must learn important lessons to survive. Which grasses are good to eat? Which animals are predators? Where are the water holes and shady places to rest? Male joeys also learn how to fight. They start by kicking and wrestling with their mothers. Older joeys practice with each other. They will spend the rest of their lives competing for a dominant position in the mob.

Did You Know . . .

A mother's milk changes as her baby develops. When the baby starts growing fur, the milk becomes richer in protein. When the joey is active outside the pouch, the milk has more fat to provide energy. A mother nursing two joeys produces a different type of milk for each nipple!

5 Kangaroos and Humans

A girl and a boy glance down a road watching for their school bus. At the sound of sudden rustling, they turn toward the nearby woods. A kangaroo and her joey stroll out from among the trees. The children have seen these two before. Dropping their books, they run over to the animals. The girl bends down and picks up the baby. Her brother strokes its belly. Soon the rumble of the bus sends the children scrambling for their books. The kangaroos head for strips of grass growing along the road. They barely glance up as the bus chugs by.

The relationship between kangaroos and humans began about 50,000 years ago. This is when people

Kangaroos delight both tourists and native Australians. They are on Australia's coat of arms and on its money.

called the *Aborigines* first settled in Australia. Europeans discovered kangaroos during their explorations of Australia in the 1600s. Both groups hunted kangaroos for their meat and skins.

When people came to Australia, they brought non-native animals with them. The Aborigines introduced the dingo, now a wild predator. Europeans brought other hunters such as foxes and cats. They also introduced rabbits and goats. Nimble goats compete with rock-wallabies for the grass that grows on stony slopes. They also force wallabies from caves where they make their homes. Rabbits take over the dens of burrowing bettongs.

European settlers changed the kangaroo's habitat in other ways. They removed trees to clear land for farming and for grazing sheep and cattle. Many forest-dwelling kangaroo species lost their homes. In the dry, central part of Australia, called the outback, ranchers have dug wells for their thirsty livestock. With more water available, the outback can support a larger number of kangaroos. During times of drought the kangaroos take precious water set out by ranchers for their sheep and cattle. Farmers also complain that kangaroos devour grasslands and crops.

This 1777 engraving is from a book describing Captain James Cook's voyage to Australia.

Photographing curious kangaroos can be difficult.

The Australian government has stepped in to address these complaints. The government allows a certain number of kangaroos to be killed each year by licensed hunters. The number is based on the size of kangaroo populations. The meat and skins are then sold. Kangaroo meat is marketed as pet food and is also eaten by people. Kangaroo skins, which are sturdy, lightweight, and flexible, are used in making running shoes and gloves.

The Australian government has set aside national parks and wildlife sanctuaries to protect kangaroos and their habitat.

Australians take great pride in their national symbol. They are making sure kangaroos thrive in their native land for years to come.

Some people object to the hunting of kangaroos. They feel that other methods should be used to control the size of kangaroo populations. Scientists have experimented with putting birth-control substances into salty soil that kangaroos lick. These substances stop kangaroos from reproducing, which helps decrease their numbers. Some farmers and ranchers electrify fences and water troughs to keep kangaroos away from crops and water. Others install noisemaking machines. The machines' sounds are disturbing to kangaroos but are barely detected by people. Some farmers simply shoot over the kangaroos' heads to scare them away from their fields. One explains that he enjoys having kangaroos around, as long as they don't eat too much of his crop.

Most Australians like living in "kangaroo country." People travel from around the world to see these unusual animals. The kangaroo has long been a symbol of Australia. It is also the symbol of national sports teams, of the Australian airline Qantas, and of products like blankets and infant carriers.

So what is the kangaroo? Is it a popular symbol, an adorable tourist attraction, a source of meat and skins, or a crop-chomping pest? The Aborigines, who have known the kangaroo the longest, have their own idea. The kangaroo, they tell us, like every animal on Earth, is our relative.

Glossary

Aborigines: The first people to live in Australia. They most likely came from Asia about 50,000 years ago.

dominant: The highest ranking male, usually the strongest, largest, and oldest one.

evaporate: To change from a liquid into a gas.

habitat: The natural surroundings of a living thing.

instinctively: Acting with inborn knowledge.

joey: A baby kangaroo.

mammal: A warm-blooded animal that has a backbone and fur or hair, gives birth to live young, and makes milk to feed its young.

marsupials: Mammals whose young are born at an early, undeveloped stage. Most marsupial females have a pouch, where young continue to grow and develop.

mob: Kangaroos of one species living in the same area.

predator: An animal that hunts and eats other animals.

species: A particular type of living thing.

tendon: A band of tissue that connects bones to muscles.

Find Out More

Books

Arnold, Caroline. *Kangaroo*. New York: William Morrow, 1987.

Burt, Denise. *Kangaroos*. Minneapolis: Carolrhoda Books, 2000.

Darling, Kathy. *Kangaroos on Location*. New York: Lothrop, Lee, and Shepard Books, 1993.

Domico, Terry. *Kangaroos: The Marvelous Mob*. New York: Facts on File, 1993.

Green, Jen. *Kangaroos*. Danbury, CT: Grolier Educational, 2001.

Markle, Sandra. *Outside and Inside Kangaroos*. New York: Atheneum Books for Young Readers, 1999.

Miller-Schroeder, Patricia. *Kangaroos*. Austin, TX: Raintree Steck-Vaughn, 2002.

Watts, Dave. *Kangaroos and Wallabies of Australia*. Frenchs Forest, N.S.W., Australia: New Holland Publishers, 1998.

Woodward, John. *Kangaroos*. Tarrytown, NY: Marshall Cavendish, 1997.

Films

Australia's Kangaroos. National Geographic Home Video, 2000.

Kangaroos. Diamond Entertainment Corp., 1995.

Kangaroos: Faces in the Mob. Green Cape Wildlife Films, 1992.

The Wonderful Kangaroo. Kodak Programs, Inc., 1988.

Web Sites

Australian Wildlife

http://users.orac.net.au/~mhumphry/austwild.html

Australian Wildlife: Kangaroos

http://www.australianwildlife.com.au/features/kangaroo.htm

Kangaroo Biology

http://www.deh.gov.au/biodiversity/trade-use/wild-harvest/
kangaroo/biology.html

National Wildlife Federation: Everything You Always
Wanted to Know about Kangaroos

http://www.nwf.org/internationalwildlife/kangaroo.html

Wikipedia: Macropod

http://en.wikipedia.org/wiki/Macropod

Unique Australian Animals

http://australian-animals.net/

Index

Page numbers for illustrations are in **boldface**.

About the Author

Judith Jango-Cohen's intimate knowledge of nature comes from years of observing and photographing plants and wildlife in forests, deserts, canyons, and along seacoasts. Titles from her thirty-four children's books have been recommended by the National Science Teacher's Association, chosen for the Children's Literature Choice List, and named a Best Children's Book of the Year by the Children's Book Committee at Bank Street College. You can find photos from her many travels at www.agpix.com/cohen.